Fully Into Ashes

Fully Into Ashes

Sofia M. Starnes

WingsPress

San Antonio, Texas
2011

Cover: Photograph by Bryce Milligan of the Great Window
at St. Luke's Episcopal Church, San Antonio, Texas. The
window was conceptualized by a committee headed by the
Rev. Joseph L. Brown; designed by Cecil Casebier, with
Henry Steinbomer, architect, and Margaret Pace, craftsmaster.

First Edition

Print Edition ISBN: 978-0-916727-70-3
ePub ISBN: 978-1-60940-021-7
Kindle ISBN: 978-1-60940-022-4
Library PDF ISBN: 978-1-60940-023-1

Wings Press
627 E. Guenther
San Antonio, Texas 78210
Phone/fax: (210) 271-7805

On-line catalogue and ordering:
www.wingspress.com
All Wings Press titles are distributed to the trade by
Independent Publishers Group
www.ipgbook.com

Library of Congress Cataloging-in-Publication Data:

Starnes, Sofía M.
  Fully Into Ashes / Sofía M. Starnes. -- 1st ed.
    p. cm.
  ISBN 978-0-916727-70-3 (pbk. : alk. paper) -- ISBN 978-
1-60940-021-7 (epub) -- ISBN 978-1-60940-022-4 (kindle)
-- ISBN 978-1-60940-023-1 (library pdf)
1. Poetry — Christian. I. Title.
PS3619.T3753 2011
811'.6--dc22
Library of Congress Control Number: 2011923674

For Bill, always

&

For the teachers of the Institución Teresiana—

especially Chuchi Pacía, first written word

Contents

First House: Find

Leaving Pompeii: Ache

The Moonlight House: Gift

First House

–Find

I am bewildered by my fall,
how the ground rose between groans and good lips,
how it hummed when the tower homed,

fully into ashes.
And all I heard, whooshed between words,
was love you, love me.

—The House That Spoke

Intercession 1

A time for keeping quiet,
A time for speaking …

—Ecclesiastes: 3

Not the attic light, but the bricks that left us asking
where the house was,

and the widow-walk.
Not the porch lamps, but the blueprint of a sunroom

and a window stripped to bone. Chanticleer.
By early dawn, the swindle of a cockcrow flew apart.

So, did death stop speaking too?
All our ladders have become: ribcage, bruise

appraisal, crackers in a can, dry root—
which is to say, a basement full of words made

tangible—
music in large cages and small rooms.

And so I turn to *voice* as sling, to *call* as latticework
of tongues

(gossips in a loft),
that breaks our fall through ink and mockingbird,

those nights we test our hand on spring, incur a rustle—
brush before abandon.

First House

Hardly a way to find the window and the lock,
the bellied casement with its screen,

ironskin of evening. We have not
mastered the equation: this remembrance

and the past, the odd aroma and a jar
of pickled mangoes. The tongue recovers

first the sugar, then the treetop,
then the fruit; one for one, what is

memory turns portent—which is good,
since we're traipsing out of doors,

out of kitchens, out of decks, into a clean
white morning. Come, see

where you were feasted in those days,
the curtains slung, the sky deliciously intrusive.

A blue fan whistled, a woman cried.
And the body *recognized*, while the portent

whispered: *might be*. Come, see where
you were born, a mother's memory restores it.

> *A pitcher trembled in the foyer,*
> *With a garland of chrysanthemums—*
> *Yellow bush around the belly.*
> *And the birds brushed on*
> *Its porcelain flew home, while she lay*
> *Wish-worn, child-bearing,*

Loving more, more—
Baby talk. The garland clipped. Thumbs
Across her knuckles in a T—
Te quiero, te amo: *words upon*
Her sweaty wrists. The achy limb-sway
Metaphored, futured into spring.

Awash

A summer out of willow skirts, green stalks
rising to our waists, the river's
skin prone, onto us—

                              the wind,
           a sprinting breath, the brushed-up
bank, a brow, and phlox as idle babies

in their beds—
                 The redbird flies,
beret and cheek and cardinal; red hub, red

hollow, red madrigal woods.
                 I'm dreaming up identities, when all
I know is reference: rib-cage, sweet-gum,

palpable season by the roots.
                       The world to heart—
what's left of Eden rarifies; the garden

mists, and I gather her blindly.
                 Rain
                 pinpoints

like a brainstorm in the yard, dazzling
with craft.
Ah, if one could write this way,

think this way—not dressed but drenching.
                 When we were young,
a woman held our hands under the tap

and shimmered through us—
the water, clear; the door, ajar; the draft, a tactile
song of clementines into the hall.

She washed us thus, all fingers sluicing equally,
giddy the skin,
true, as a soft thumb's dimple . . .

    We always brim over,
before we're memory—
      the way a summer brims. Leafing.

The House That Spoke

Here is a task to undertake—
let's build a house out of a sigh,
to be, through memory, a language: brick-work,
brick-word, rumors from swung rattan,

spelling out our tales.
And the sigh will be the rust stain on the wall,
a pipe's great story which we failed to hear
in summer patches.

If the house were grander, garrulous,
we might forget those *aaahs...* of rooted pitch,
shingles that squandered foreign rain,
vocal squares—white, whitest

where a door sings glories.
And we'll say: the sigh was a pre-Babel thing,
heart-awe before that ancient hour, when
we gaped skyward, gleaning why, for how long,

and at whose nostalgic bidding.
Aaah... the sigh will become a drawn-out dream,
for beasts of wonder, for wings,
for people leaving secretive houses, stuttering—

Why not say, simply?

> *I am bewildered by my fall, how*
> *the ground rose between groans and good lips,*
> *how it hummed when the tower homed,*
>
> *fully into ashes.*
> *And all I heard, whooshed between words,*
> *was love you, love me.*

Fiction

Our God is in heaven,
He creates whatever he chooses.

Upon the stage, God's people seemed consoled: their
soldiers were no longer flesh-and-bones, but extras from
a dinky distant town; their scars were pastry, they were
sharing crusts, a cherry picker's loot in thin disguise.

An actor waited by a balcony, his leather-hair entangled,
a fickle shell precarious on his hip. They watched in
thrall; click-launch-it-go; the devil of a season turned to
ghost.

Come, children, do not cry for them,
these people are not real;
their bruises come from resins off a tree—
the magic world of artists.
Look there—
the magic world of artists.

———

The word fleshes then fades. Is this the best they do, the
reassurances they give? That histories will wake and fall
asleep behind a silver blanket? Their screenplay's out of
reach; their author, swift and lambent: lost belief.

———

Once, God the Father tended to his son, who winced
before the blood-clots on the fur, the birthright switch,
the dying. He would not be consoled; he burnt his eyelash
gazing at their ash, and squirmed and wondered nightly.

And so, the Father said....

Come, Jesse, do not cry for them;
these people are not real—
the stemcell and the rose,
the amoeba in a river,
the opossum lying mute across the tar,
the ribcage, like a harp of heaving bones,
the children grown,
the thud-thud of an ancient man, departing.
We made them up—all these,
creations of a dizzy afternoon.
See? There slips our garland on their globe;
now comes their golden End—

But neither god could bear
to pull the daylight from them.

"Are They Thinking About the Grape?"
(Francois Boucher, Chicago Art Institute)

Outlasting

And this is where I paused—
      I'd left the dark and lacquer
of the stairs, the shadow-head triangular
      and steep, and come to a Boucher:

young boy pining for girl with a grape.
      Two children, veining into a life,
no further—and for our eyes, they
      flirt, year after year.

Unlikely, don't you think?
      After all, the leaves outside, closer
to us and to living, tally our summers
      tied to our earthly affairs. A siren

wails, cablights zip and unzip nightly;
      our bones, achy gossipers, hazard
onto an edge.
      And who cares if a boy's love lingers?

The crowds cringe, beads of creation
      strewn about; a man and a woman
brave each other on a bench. Once in a while,
      the spare light spares them,

and the world shimmers on.
      What would it take to tamper with light
and be lasting?
      Ah, this is where it fails:

where a painter paints the future as a wish
          and stops before it,
stops a purpling grape, the perfect, levied wrist,
          before their fingers fasten,

          and a life shivers through.

A Might-be Summer

Teach us to count up the days that are ours.

Another serving, please,
of days we left. And nature comes around—

blonde, motherlike—moirés the table slowly
with a cloth, hesitates at the doorway....

Another serving of things someone
said, dazzling with what might be,

was not: the rich tan
of an afternoon, the solid air still smoldering,

the yellow cake with icing in our thumbs,
to eat away bright, brightly.

And no one knows how August crisps, jinxes
the roots of hair a pungent amber.

Embers.
How do you spend your day? They ask years

later, and everywhere the word hangs, hangs
between.   *Writing,* I say.

A dozen birdhouses descend under their trees,
all different, with gargoyles, needling

spires, white lattice wood. They dance
to eucalyptus.   A dozen children

play around the rocks—this only
I—and anyone—regret, eventually: our flat

words insufficient in the morn, our dry aprons
intact, the smell of resurrection

crusting. Little hands scuttle away
from unacquainted pockets. I fill them now,

late evening between poems,
confessing only a part: A child is what she is;

not the day,
nor the doubt my word careens against—

> There I go now, forgetting.

"Habbakuk" or "Lo Zuccone"
(Donatello, Museo dell'Opera del Duomo)

Adolescent

A heart worth knowing
is a heart to fear:
a boy, stretched out

in the porch, biting off
his nails.
He's shaved his head—a ripe

zuccone, bald
as Donatello's prophet.
Non finito.

        Under clouds,
his column leans imperiled,
in between tank-top and

tunic, on the wind
of furious artists—
        I see him there,

like the old inmates of stone,
vein-cages
taunting and near,

while no one touched them.
I think how beautiful
the boys are, freed

from their quarry, and
the fathers who raise them,
heads borne on strong

shoulders,
beneath temperate lamps.
            But now, there's this boy,

shivering in the rain,
a tree-frog on his lap, ghostly.
            Above the eaves,

a sudden storm wakens,
whitens the porch.
Light rivets the roof,

sends him up, sparkling,
while his frog leaps.
He starts at thunder:

at fulfillment.
            Oh, it comes easy
for the cloud and the sky's

smock, the green beast and
its retina, the stone
garnering a face.

Work me into non finito.
It comes hard, hardest for the boy,
who knows that a squash

sweetens, while the soil reeks,
that the heads lie, spoiling,
that his heart must sculpt

into branches.

Distances

The world transcendent,
Mrs. B. defined, gingerly:
a little beyond.
        The soul sweet-talks
its way into the throng

of lung, ribcage, hip. The lips
are doorsill, in and out;
I do not know which-way.
        What kills a rose?
My nephew asked, a young boy

living in the world,
hung to a thing called cellular.
        Ah, the real cell, a livid
child, cub of the little beyond,
dances its animal dance,

before something scurries
through our brain,
pollen-rich and budding:
the loveliest heart,
human, hurrying up its blood.

Should I not call this
God's rose, mid-summer agony
we loved, cannot love, might
love forever?   Alive!
The rose beside the paper box—

alive, after the beetles
gorge, under their hard green
backs, whatever does not quicken
far enough, deep enough
into the soil.

What kills the rose?
The bussing forth—
kiss me, she says, *I say* ... abreast,
with garden pleasure.
A wasted whiff, miffing, strikes

heart, a little beyond.

Lola's Window

The call to make-believe, later forbidden,
a liturgy of ghosts—
        Every night she settled near the window,

Capiz comb and wrinkle on the wood.
The moon dimpled to zero on her lap, remade
eclipse, tight-lip to a sun's invasion.

And in that shade, cool and somnolent,
her memory grew certain.
        Once she was a child in a resplendent

room, hoping for an annunciation—
drive of wings down and inward, ballet
in the weave of a blind.

There she'd hear the angel's liquid claim,
        Come where the brilliance is yours;
        come, carry off the cry.

Released at last of all painstaking growth,
of hands out of jackstones and sipa,
out of the box-like patintero she could not play,

not being swift enough.
Only the god of the white room—
        This you do and only this,

        for your patio of light.
Midnight dropped its spell under her eaves,
nugget of those years when the moon always

reached, always rescued.
        Loss is an old but ample word for ghost;
        prize is the better word for angel.

La Flor de Tía Peting

Not quite a resurrection,
the foredawn and a woman
at her bath.

Who hears her humming?
The heat rosaries the steam
hushward,

all in good time—
and the wet curl on her nape
careens into a hyacinth.

Why not into a poem,
closer to finger-prod and
breast-perfume,

to penances that perished
on her lap?
Flood to flood. *La flor*

de tía Peting—
a name to plant and press—
pinning antiquity on the grass.

Should we unpair them?
The flower, nearly a word;
the woman

always cottoned
in her chair, her laundered
oldness,

cloak to us.
The slippers rub her toes;
the music scurries.

No one explains
the gift of a redundant life
to abandoned life,

of rumors, codas—
lip-deeds that undone
become become become . . .

A memory sneaks off,
into the half-smile
of a room where she dresses,

combs, powders her arms
with stories—
Who hears her in the come

come coming yard?
No one—
but for the uncatch

of our window, *something*
like a hearsay hyacinth,
the white wood

hum hum humming.

How They Survive

I desire mercy, not sacrifice . . .

Bold-green and unbred,
this nettle-skin of upstarts, and like

a pimply rash the loveless
pigeon-weed. Our backwoods itch

and hatch—a way of thriving—
berries that marble

in spray, and in a dewy under,
crickets rub their music out of reach.

A cat prowls at the edge, paws
sticky with old tiger humors, sparing

them—but not the up-ended
turtle with blotchy head, the snowy

crow (too pale, too pale), the pebble-
eyed somnambulate. . . .

Is this the story
of brave-or-lose, all's fair in love and

war, fate of a species on the verge
of scandal?   Is this

about a limping race, a temple licked,
a runt amid the trampled rushes?

Emboss the youngest skin; come,
press the face of mercy against it.

All the same, when burrows clear and
hares abuse new colonies, a sparrow,

eyeing its odds, drops from the beech—
Think of her eggs out of reach,

think a mere scuffle in thatch—
the damp, doable stalemate.

Provinces

The Lord is my shepherd . . .

Imagine a province with nothing you've
owned—shepherds and rucksacks,

mustard and figs, fence-
posts and pastures, valley of death.

Picture cedars and slingshots, a pocket
of beans, knotted sandals—

further downhill, the pink of a lamb no one seeks.
In this story (and others) they

tell us of these—an inn and a portico,
temple and dome: upheavals... the hazardous

eyes of a boy close to swine,
hung jury of a father in drapery robes,

the red
ring he surrenders.

And the stories have more
of the unknown: a river that licks what is other-

wise dry, the flap of a fishtail
in stone, always food, always given.

What is it about psalms
that converts them to tales of *our* weeds,

the brown chicory pulled from our drives,
our blank corrals?　　　　What holds

things—consolation, or garden, or hope?
What returns, blowing over the twilight-gold

pollen we bear to our tombs, ache for angels?
          We have left a dark Plymouth still idling,

our fog on its glass, a pure dent
in the backrest—the little we owned of a father,

a road, old communions.
          Seven times we will wash away grist

from the slab, rub the name, clean-sleeve
over; seven times we'll hear, coming, the bleat

and the scuffle of lambkins.
                    Seven times the custodian—

or shepherd—will wait for us, sign for us,
one by one: *Hija!* My child…

                    Are you lost? Are you tarrying?

Leaving Pompeii

—Ache

Intercession II

The Home Front

Fresh tar and the men entranced, remaking what I've seen
at evening nineteen years. We change so slightly—dogwoods

and a lima-shaped bed of coreopsis, and the cone-heads left
from black-eyed Sues. Muggy or cool—our God is in a green

robe, balancing whatever season in his palm. His goods
confuse, at times; his goods amuse. But in this twilight-theft

of hour, we sit endangered. We have a list of thoughts and hazy
profiles pulled toward extinct; a dove-tail disappearing—*dear*

child, hold the kite's song in your fist—and a rush of air remin-
iscent of alive. Once done, the men fill up the hole, a crazy-

quilt, coal-stitch and wire. I think: so close to conflicts, we're
guardians, all; we set our roadblocks, shield our candescent skin.

It is as though a household knocker rapped: Keep close to home;
Keep home. As if a distant continent crept into my room.

The Death of the Piper Pilot

Another Way to Leave

The breeze settles, the rain settles, the day
wanders forth in promise,

while the catbird cracks its loot, bristles
the alyssum. And I watch

(the story's sketchy) how the pilot who mis-
matched the brittle cove is laid to rest.

       Ah… these lines open with death,
when they shouldn't.

"Blessed" is a better word, "Hear" and
"Heart" and "Praise": "Deliver him, O God."

But the dying holds its place where I have
found it.

    Tight and tidy, far too tidy, shut
    and silent, far too mute. Dry and cold-
    eyed, far too common in the dark—

Is death wicked?
       When it clicks out of a mouth, abrupt

and barren, when it singles out a heart-plot,
clips its shoot, clamps desire for quick

nocturnal thinning; when it trips in, steals up
closely, whispers to a young—

    Not too tidy, not too mute;
    here's a slack knot for your heart,
    winds to come my wind outlast.

Was it thus? That the pilot heard his call,
too blue, too mellow

to be godless: Lamb in wolf—
that a full life, warm around his earlobes,

rushed.

At a butterfly birthing ground,
near Chapultepec, Mexico

The Fret of Memory

In our guidebook, a slope;
in the caption, a note
about dismantled monarchs
surrendering purses
        to the ambit of slugs,

to be slurped daily, nightly
in marvelous dank, below large
unattainable hazes;
        in that place of a last kiss
extended, the extent

of an insect divided in halves—one
        borne bodily
in coal-veins, areolas,
over phosphorous rocks;
                the other held

back: like the tang
in a mouth or a cavern;
like the hang of a vanishing truth.
        Oh, the fret of a poem
and its motions, why

a memory extends it, why
        it seeks out the half-verse,
the half-world,
alit and afloat all at once,
the half-amorous

mock, and the cocked ear encircling
some forgotten
           occurrence.
A migration of losses flocks
over the page: pinpoint deaths—

           And the word that was wander
and rest
is now *Thing*.

                    —*for Marcia W.-S.*

Leaving Pompeii

We pause to celebrate it all—
      the candles glossed to candy-
stubs, a parrot purchased
      for its Latin talk, the daylong
proud hibiscus on a stem,

      and more:
our neighbors' sidings painted
      oyster white, fresh mulch
in levees between rose & rose,
      the crawly-creepy bicycles

across, children that learn
      rotation on their wheels.
We celebrate the trickle, & the man-
      made lake whose bottom
leaked all summer, & the drip

      that keeps autumns awake,
gold almonds on our sheets.
      (Ah, crinkled stiff; we have
loitered too long.)
      Dust settles swiftly over

wax & toy, the shutting tiara of petals
      by our doors, the bicycles
left leaning. Our parrot picks
      at drifting grains & snorts.
Before we can withdraw, a friend

      a drops by, tucks scent &
crescent in our rooms, then urges: *go*—
      The night is now a stranger,
dark and lean: guest
      to the heart's abundant feast.

How Things Are Saved

Our moments in enduring
rings, our loss in stages—chestnut
young, baby gold, bark over bark,

mid-autumn.
We could be living
the life of a tree, orchard or woods,

if we would wrap things cleanly,
quietly.
Look at the ivory under their hides,

naïve as a child.
Come inside.
The window holds impermanent

eyes: blue drapes, blue swags, drop-
down memory
of moonsurge and sun.

                    Separate at birth,
we learn life—every minute
of it—as freeze and sublimation apart;

we stare back at left-over
reds, wondering how in the world
we'll move on without them.

Where are the stems and their snippets,
the thimble-like buds, spools
that predate living?

Where is the silkworm whose silk
eternally trickles?
                    Every generation

weaves its cloak, womanly:
       hold this in your heart.
Vast, variegated greys tangle luminous

tassels, tease up children to come,
clumps of unruliest hair.

Marye's Heights

Ashes are the food that I eat—

That afternoon we walked all
over them, with sparrows nibbling hay,

heartbeats counting hedges,
loft and hem—and only halfway there:

> *Once there was a winter and a war,*
> *once upon their footprints lay a spark,*
> *stories from a woman's yard...*

Her hollyhocks prickled with frost,
a hungry fire hissed;

toward it the feverish wandered.
　　　The woman served cardamom

tea (so the story unfolds), one
fist clenched in her apron—her ovum,

her planet, her world—dim savable
room, which she saved. She gave

everything else.
　　　Ages later, the kitchen holds these:

jars of beets, ears of corn, bread in pewter—
all ready to eat

with a ghost's possibility, *look into her eyes...*
that Mrs. S. stayed, pouring on, while

the boys dyed her lime-hill—
O grass grown uncountable, cindering young

consuming far more than her stretch of leaves,
or ours, unleafed—

their short stories late through the night.

Migrations

Peel and pare: a summer episode—
     and we walk into the cool and
common backyard,
     to a dusk that dims
the foreignness of shade

     —and to *heart*, where we, too,
at times disheartened,
     break a mandarin for that soft,
familiar naveling of suns....
     A fruit guarantees a space, lush

appointment, pungent segment, bitter-
     kind spatula—a fruit wears
intact the integument of womb,
     of a homestead we pried open
leaving genesis beneath,

     all those stories of our fathers
and their trees, our mothers' hands,
     the sweet globes plumping.
Our thumbs are licked, the pits forgone;
     the world shudders off its skin.

Tell me, darling:
     couldn't we, as heelbones press,
stumble *there*—a heaven *there*,
     where our apricots, far-fetching
over a neighbor's plot, tumble in pairs,

     or where geese, no longer northern,
heart-locked in their lost migrations,
     flock? What a sight—
if bones shifted, if as gold seeds hurtling,
     we bore homesick pods.

Vespers in ICU

Peak and valley, star-flower rise—
hunter's trickle;
a tulip poplar braves out

on a flat evening—
       and the task of living in a room
fleshes into fickle wrens

inside a box.
They chirp—the night dips low; they
chirp—the bird

is my good fortune,
strong music for your breath.
       But who will word this muscle-

song forever?
The poem meanders to the sill,
out of sight; sunlight arrows through mid-

frost, the patio reddens
under redder jaws, and children
scramble to the edge, in a high-pitched

gaggle.
Downwind, a woman takes the wrong
key to her car; this

is the only danger for her now,
the metal clot under her knuckles, small
Lucifer steel.

       The afternoon slinks far off
with its rust, mild crust
of unweaponed hazes.   Inside,

a heart pumps: peak
and valley, a skyline peril in moonlight
paneling—

       the night's shivery gift.

The Dance After

Fox Trot for a Convalescent

This evening   the precocity of stars,
fox trot and haze
galaxying out, meteors kissing

with the cold
all over them. They dance through Mars,
beet-faced and bold,

not quite bellicose, in a tantrum
perhaps, or in hunger
for a peach from a different

planet.   They sweep over,
near-collide
against perfume and throat, wind-strum…

They wear our terrified faces.
          Come and dance, you ask, a vein
bent wistfully on your temple,

the trumpet deep.
                    Come and dance.
And not an evening hurts; not a perfect pair,

fondling and hugging in ample
heavens, races
as swiftly as the blood, thin

and joyous, between us.
                    The terror
dares our share of entropy: leaf-cut, clot-

chance, mute fault under the music.
　　　　It leaps out of our skin
and fingertips, careens

into the night.
　　　　And the nights turn mystic
for a while, risky for a while, light and blue

and blissing. *Come and dance.*
The days press—mystified, heartwhole.

The Rood of Jesse

On July 10, 2001, a shark attacked a 10-year-old Mississippi boy near Pensacola, Florida—two months before September 11.

I   The Coastline
    7/10

Fine eyelash moon through the antiseptic
window, and he blinks; crib

of a thousand months gone by; his eye
dilates a dream—salt-still

in this uncommon child.
The stillness is not his but God's.

            I picture God
a roamer on the beach, his shoulders bare

as a blue sky, blue-black bruise
over the planet. And every bruise repeats itself,

maps his torsos and legs, sore veins
running. This time, his bones have taken

the full brunt;
all over him, godhurt.

            Eternity in the wound:
there is no point in asking why

the abandonment, the slippage of mercy
at the jaw.   Eternity at the intersect of hurt,

thigh-stump and knee-sigh, sting
and burn, the clover

that cramps for a bee, the dandelion huffing in dry
grass, crossbow of nests for survival—

A nightingale drops from its high perch,
slips into the shark's angle: *sing!*　　Will heaven

refuse this voice?
A moonless squeeze aches over, pulses, pleads.

II　His Room
　　7/20

In our limb, his limb-loss, a tingle in the thumb.
While we wait, red wine

courses out of grapevines into us—we, the carafe,
we, the glass transparency

and the nick, veeing.
God is good, the harvest says, wherever the rain

nourishes; yet it washes someone's grenadines
away.

God is good. The porch-rail ribbons
into scarves,

yellow afloat on a mad river,
nights awaiting the adjuster with our young.

God is good.
We cannot wander, rich or lithe, in isolation. Daylight

loves in clusters, purple plums
and shriveled prunes: the same enormous summer.

And life glorifies its feat,
spring or flood, shark or gosling. And it blushes,

and it prickles,
and it simplifies our life. Ask no more.

Jack-be-nimble in the eyelid of the child,
and an urchin in his palm; dance him now.

The boy winces in his sleep, frets
against the window light, the unrecognized defeat

of a fish—
God is good; the blood laces up his arm.

III His Mother
     8/10

Ah, a woman at the stove-lamp
of her kitchen, stirring lentils,

gold-oil on the wafered broth.
Thus the olive gave, is giving.

She has come home for her wait,
while God squeezes,

but the breath is hers to heave,
pondered with his sigh.

Now the woman serves a meal
in the Edenic resurrection

of her role: *I will feed you, from*
my hoards and my disclosures,

from my presses and my cellar,
from the pickled jars in rows,

shelves below the sun; I will feed
you from my new unlabeled

crates of screw-neck glass, apples
and night raisins rolled in nuts.

I will feed my child forever
where he lies,

with the drip, the serum pouch—
sweet syringe, my baby—

And God separates her fruits
with the sweetspot of his thumb.

IV His Sky
    8/20

In the grand arena of things—
all because the moon is

one in a memory of moons, all because she
mystifies grandly

whether we have stepped on her or
not, flagged her or not, bagged a rosary or not,

stones out of her aprons.
          When the men left her, nostalgic

for their mists of rhododendron,
she became small, smaller,

one loose button in a black Madonna's blouse,
hanging in the night.

       One of many—
And it makes the telling sad.

         One of many, many poems,
which is why we dream the scene larger:

not the moon, but the moons after,
not the bloom, but the salvation of the rose-

gardens of the world,
not the shadow, but a giant bending over,

blueing darkness into, out of us.
               We hope God—

Not the child, but the fate of generations
wishboning the wombs, for a chance.

One of many—
      How the zigzag stakes his temple, how

the insufficient ghost throbs his heart.

V   His Eyes
    9/10

Some whispers cannot rise above a war,
so listen hard: the boy has seen

what boys desire. I'd say a dinosaur, a flute,
the leafy light on leaf-thin chips,

the cheesy sun in crumbs, and at his wrists,
a woman's thumb, perusing.

What was the reason he knew?
A red scar bled under the moon, possessed itself

over Mama's head, and there she was, intimate
as wound, as his raw moment unpassing.

The fixed beachline and the blue fairground,
a mere blood-pint away, loosened.

Now he sees her under the blind, a Corinth grape
in a bowl's virtues, plump pick

out of their backyard mesh. Deep down,
a creature; for every desire, always a creature.

Our Eyes
9/11

Crater eyes—we, too, have squinted through our
wishes for a sweet mouth in a wreckage,

a body's dimpled flower, another life—
Come, come, Lord, give us another life,

hope for the forklift. We wish someone would climb
piece-meal into our eyes. To see is to select.

Isn't that Lazarus over the glistening steel, covering
his sores?

Look! *Here, here I am? Can't you see I made it?*

What They Never Knew

Vespers; September 10

The habit of redress, awareness
as forewarning, afterthought—
and meteorites in place, blinking

to a pink, inevitable dawn. *What did
Jeremy see?* That night, they took
their usual walks. Out of the loam,

a turtle rose, the graveyard
on its back, a legend of criss-cross—
they might have said: imagine living

underneath our past. *What did Todd
whisper home?* The rain began.
They stood out on each porch and tried

to enchant it, forgetting every storm
behind. They never could, so thick
their memories of apples plucked

in gales, of pearl-eyes on the screens,
and lizards finger-cold on moonlit
swags. *Where did Mark spend the night?*

Tomorrow they will lose the doors,
and duffle bags with stories on their backs;
a blast will peel the steel, the vinyl off—

a fortunetelling without yarrow strands.
*What made Lou wink at dreams above
his bed?* The vivid ash reveals mere

bone, mere flesh. *Did Tom await this?*
Theirs was the threat that slept, rose,
differed them full, forthcoming. Theirs,

also, the unwarned: the brave benevolent
hour, when—a latch before, a link
before—they lived, half-kissed upon.

Safe

Observe the innocent, consider the honest,
for the man of peace will not lack children.

In the homestretch of summer,
on the lazier greens of a land,
where geography, barely a nectarine

seed in our palm, turned into carbon
creases, wrinkles of a star—
                    At the mound

of a wreckage, we looked—oh, so weary—
for bones in old daylight,
for tenderfoot bodies,

now nimbler, now lighter, arrived.

Wander forth, coming child, give
this sunset of people your tenderest pulse:
for the evenings are saved by the young.

            Could it finally be—
we, recovering baskets and chairs,
a porch-rail, a lamp, a rim of geraniums

in bloom; in the backyard,
well into the twilight, our sons counting
strikes.

        Could a summer be this?
Sight that shimmers all swing and ellipse
into swing of an arm,

a herringbone dimple that draws in
the hide—crack-clamor of ash—
the magnificent bow where things vanish.

Ah, to call landscape, love:
love for sacrifice squeeze,
for younger and louder,

for a heart-and-wrist mound,
where we seek out redemption,
as foothold—

on pathway, on grass—
never far from a house and a chair,
a porch-rail, a wick: a delayed homesick arc,

children startling.

"Duelo A Garrotazos"
(Francisco de Goya, Museo del Prado)

The House in Ruins

He digs a trap, scoops it out,
but he falls into the snare he made himself.

I

You look over my shoulder, eyes set on the exhibit
overhead; it's wringing out the heavens....

We live off wounds, don't we?
How will the world sustain this—

Today, half our body's buried in the earth,
as Goya's giants, whose clubs rained thorn and destiny

on their heads,
whose knees were water-logged as cypress knees,

and swampy.
A townline hampered the horizon: twilight eaves, thistle,

and the invisible spire,
while duelers dueled, sunsetting all at once.

Where is their beauty now, this close, calf-high
in mud, the assailed head slumped

against the assailant's shoulder?
Whose idols grace the land with midnight losses?

Life clings to their sash-cloths, whips and hunches mor-
tals
into one—

Half our body understands the meet, baffles
the blow yet takes it; half splices the incoming

wind, shivers fate out of a riddle.
Hour on hour, the moon soaks the weaponing wood.

II

Come, see the *Duelo* again: this time, the storm's
ajar, one elbow high against the blue, arms flung

in double-ecstasy transfixed—and at the tips, garrotes.
Not one of us denies it: split-oaks of a late

revenue's offense, shades marring the moss equally;
and the men's panic at having outgrown

the house—
gigantic loss, gigantic love, into the ultimate—

Livid in our heartache
is their blood, their fever is familiar as a bull-run and

hot black coffee and *anís,*
and the need to be this drastic halfway through a life.

Half-lit, the sunny roofs *we* trimmed,
the roofs *we* nailed, roofs no longer coping with pink

flowering walls
from where our homeplot measures.

Mercy, O Lord, on us;
mercy on these children you carefully toweled,
certain we were muddied and would again

muddy our limbs, leveling.
Mercy on the waste caking our heels—
You flake it, because dirt before death is unseemly,
because it counts only
how cleanly out of, into your house, we come.

The Moonlight House

—Gift

Intercession III

Almost a lip-read beyond
    fastened panes: rain falls,
visual. What word to echo on gray
    tortoise days of slow
neglect, slow regard? I am arriving
    mutely to where You
are, shadow of the stunted rose,
    the undestroyed flower.

Stunted? Surely You do this
    with a summer end in sight,
garden of no sequoias,
    where nothing towers.
You do not tower either, or high-
    hung, scrutinize the shock
of spring, stupefied under glass
    pebbles.   Yet,

You are enormous—
    like the blush-burdened myrtle
with its month of rain, sedge-
    bound, sedge-tasting
over the pruned rose.
    Which of them, rose or myrtle, set
halfway, finally will point:
            here, wait here?

Wet as the evening, over-wet, dark
    as the hour, under-dark: You swell,
shrink, grow, bend, leave me, ah…
    flecked stammel on the ribs. Tell me.
Are these rose markings
    from Your ever-making rose?

Nightlife

The moon dissolves to mist
and flower; the window balances the outside dark

against a single lamp—
and underneath, a rose. Some nights, I know

three things: *the being rush,*
bone sequence, hide and blood, bliss of these rudiments,

from them to make a life.
                        And then, some slower

things: *the being wait*, a portal, mouthful, ache;
the knob that clicks comes loose; the hinge that stalls

holds hard.   Pause, pause—
The evening brings the undisguise of things:

the bowtie stars, the myrtle crook still blooming,
humped beside the drive;

the moonlight satisfies the alcove glow of what I know.
                        The being pluck,

the toughest being of all, out of the garden lush,
ten thousand reds, ten thousand fickle golds, toadstools

on grass. At last, the unequal rose
climbs on the bow-blade clip, a summer-seize.

            I do not fear the many from which I come.
            I do not fear the many to which I go.

Some nights, a single look for everything I lose,
a single hope

by which I'll candle back.
A nipple dribs its moon, the moonbeam dries, lipborne

into a child.
Between the moon and rose, the hourglass.

Generations

It happened thus: a woman's shiver
under a veil's surface, translucent hand,

pull of thread up and above a froth's turmoil;
a woman's hour shearing

off, all the way along her incandescent skin,
as when the moon follows its skin

through cloud and star-burst.
It happens thus: day breaks in the crater

of her throat, where marvel lasts, midnight towed
through things outlasting;   day breaks—

like the bird that pinpoints morning,
or the celebrating blue that quicks the quietness.

Somewhere else, a wine glass
splinters in a sink, Burgundy on the thumb, signet

of death for the one hunted;   elsewhere, too:
there's a quail under a tree, wincing

back to a god's lap in a jacket of pine needles.
And the woman, fully aware, dozes wisely—

giver, giveable.   Ah, both love
and love-worn shiver happen still: others

leave, all guests, all simple sallow faces.
The veil assembles moon and lungful in a room,

where light peaks over the bedposts.
Stay with me, she says; *our god is waiting.*

The world creeps homeward on her temples.

The Dresser, on a Milky Morning

—After the death of an optic nerve

O things, the way they must, at last, be seen,
debted to dying and to birth,
to gossamer equations of the sun, to tulle that teases

for the blue it hides, the quintessential wake.
       This is no longer how they etch their lives,
sprung up as moss or mushroom after a nightlong rain

I never saw, swift-coming.
Here they bend. Here they become,
Here they dance toward my open hand, half-meeting.

       I did not see the felt hats
       and the greys before,
before things crawled or hunched or crept in trenchcoats,

undercover agents—
       What's your mission; what's your metal mark?
The longest shadow will become a staff;

the inching hour in the hourglass will drop,
upon a vein's cessation.
                   Who would have thought I'd travel

all this way one night, to seek out hostages.
I rose to this: a milky dresser rescued by a jar, its dome-
head only gleaming. For a prize, my own appall

at love and seizures....   O the lock
that no one, no one seeks to open.

Winter Sight

A host of snow-anemones, intact;
a lost nerve winters in the eye,
and every word is
squint:
eventually, the world returns in squints.

Goldfinches
quiet with the year;
I turn to hear them—
for they are within fingers traipsing down
a cheek, the left side

of a jaw astir in a spare garden.
Of all our senses:
let there be light—
shall we defer to hushes?
Morse-taps out of rehearsals in the dark?

I hear a bandurria trebling;
the steel fret warms, and the palm
pleases—
until it, too, goes, candidly:
as taste and waft, candy-whiff and candy-

bite, taffy that clung to a child's
palate forever.
Forever? The eye races, spring-
time belief, lately coming,
out of which we were called saints.

Blessed are those who have not seen.
And who'll see then?
After backyard and strum, odor and saucer
of feast, the clearing of a throat
before a symphony—

A pin drops.
Somewhere, a tumbler of words,
a porch where the goldfinches flitter…
voices
for whatever a look chases.

At the gravesite of James and Dolley Madison,
near Charlottesville, Virginia

The Monument Restorer

Between storms,
an obelisk, a man, and the oils
of a late sun, streaming. He toils
away in the heart-cavity
of a field. A yard or so

from our ankles,
he soft-brushes the dead.
Lion-mane, luminous head;
hands, bristly as paws, tease up
the earth: five years in still

company.
      They're everywhere—
foot over flat foot, hair
wisp on hair, shoe buckle and
loosed linen: Sheol, Sheol.

Lord, how we bury, bless,
commend them to oak groans
and wonder: the universe owns.
      Could it be otherwise?
We, swallowing the world, it

and the withering stars,
the carbon dissolution of a place
so intended. Once out of the race—
we, with a brush on the bricks,
leveling ages.

Sweethearts and weeds,
the man and his broom,
the obelisk and the small room
under, where no one lies,
sleeps, waits. I'd swear

a lost locket appears simply
from loving—gold in the crook
of his arm where dusk leaks. Look!
Full are the man and the field,
full are we under the sun.

The Scarf

Human life . . . a mere puff of wind.

A lease of cloud, the afternoon's a scarf—
a lightweight thing to write
about.

The moment is not ponderous
at all, so I shall deal with nicknames
for a change: Russ for rust,

and Beet for red,
Mahytab for the moon-face of a girl.
          What might become the nickname

of a god?
The sober boy looks up, over a scroll:
I love my father's business. . . . He responds

to Solomon, or Jesse, or Davy—or son.
          Dusk molts over a transept
          in a church, finch-like,

and one hopes
it could chirp, and fly,
and waver daintily availing of our skin.

A small thing.
          We'll take a final
trip this spring, to see a father's chestnut

eyes, to know his business.
          We'll chatter needlessly
about the fuzzy hairstyle of a niece,

the coral dress, the blue pumps for the visit.
                    We'll walk into a liturgy,
where everything will downsize

for a while:
birth   sin   death   salvation—
down to the pretty mystery

of a dress, the silkworm's forecast,
fore-gauzing of joy,
that business of a scarf.

My father tucks
a white luminous robe around himself—
not crowned, not wept—

a small verb: merely dozing.

—Antonio Memije Molina, in memoriam

The Armoire

Save your people . . . save your heritage . . .

White lint and grey cloth, or moth on moth,
the closet opens

its overlap of living
things on things thought lifeless.

The cuff that idled around her wrist, the clicking
belt and sandals, slim

chevron straps and Cuban-heels, a little
awkward, a little dreamy . . .

chotis in the night.
They danced to this, then sidled back to the clear

divide, their throats alive,
their trinkets lifeless: earbobs

and brooch, the button-wink on his left lapel—
their hands—the clasp

on a sequin purse, slick paper lanterns.
                         Dense as a thicket,

this armoire-mix,
my mother's blonde day in chantilly, the shape

of slippers and the shape of dawn,
slipping.

In the bedside drawer, her rosaries.
                         It comes to this: to save

a people is to save their things.
Don't, don't tremble. Listen to me—

Listen to her amble beyond the door, coffer
of ashes under her arm—

and no one stops her.
Listen to the wish-wind mazing

the wall, where she nods, smiling.
Her longing levers

on lifeless things; she leaves them for us.
The closet heaves: sleeve-

lengths, wave-lengths, *Aves* in seeds, biding.
Flax-spoils of skin blow on the beads—

no, never lifeless.

Carmen Gómez-Arnau de Molina, in memoriam

All Souls Day

I'll tell you about the children,
when we've cleaned the dusty, slumber prayer

from the stone: *rest in peace; may you sleep in the Lord*—
But, no; nothing is restful about stars, or

fragments of a star, flints out of the universal hip,
reflecting.   That day, we gathered

by the crosses, unflowering stops that were
like livid irises of skin, except they never scarred.

Next to them, we set our baskets, bronzed, our supper
things. November sunlight, sunlit Day of Souls.

And then we ate: a cup of chick-peas and a sprig
of tender spinach for the soup; an egg, simmered and

diced, the drizzle of an olive—green and gold; young
legume, baby leaf, and spawn.

> *Is this how dying days bring days,*
> *how picnics keep alive our morning dead,*
> *with candid taste-and-see's amid their bones?*

I'll tell you about the children in a while, when they're
through slurping, tittering around. The broth

will soak their thumbs, leaves will gossip into chorus
grass, and every blade will tremble.

I'll tell you. Everywhere, the children will jump, jump,
unstoppable—wouldn't you?

Forever full—a further morsel crumbling.

The House That Bled

I

On Thursday, the vein quivered and
burst, its aurora imperiling

her temple's alleys. Imagine
the body's accesses this way: a settlement here,

there, the hilly mazes, begonias,
which the drivers ignore,

and prickly hollies hugging the walls.
Half-a-mile away, an intersection frets, but that

has little to do with the baby bawling
in an upstairs room, or the collie sniffing the rose,

or the mulchbed rising—
hazardous home, where she falls.

> *The vein leaked, and it flooded her hall,*
> *it threatened her words, and it squinted*
> *her light, it rose-shed her spring,*
>
> *and it wet the roots totally. The fall*
> *in her voice, unperplexed, sore, convinced,*
> *did not query the reddening*
>
> *drop of a cherry on her lap,*
> *this early attempt to remind her that He*
> *always was. And she thought, I'm in God's*
>
> *fingers now, at the end of the trap,*
> *in the ever unsellable lot, with a tree oddly*
> *in bloom, the sapling away from the floods.*

Someone built a house there, for the red
fruit that trembled incessantly, for the car-hum

a backwood away that clogged
and unclogged, strummed the pickets, for the bustle

enduring beyond the aurora in the mud.

II

Dreamy-eyed or dozing,
she must delay the recreation of her skin:

> *smooth would mean forgetful, relief*
> *would be the negative of rose,*
> *thimble of a thorn, a pink well*
> *closing up after a tornado, recalling*

nothing. We fear yet love our scars.
                    As artisans

we're drawn to storied houses, to strip and
tell their stock of wood,

armlock of newer plaster.
We know that someone notched, nicked,

blistered their beams and mantles,
until the white gypsum hung.

          Houses withstand their centuries,
double-rooms and double tales, luster

and bristle inside-out, wished-back
wounds hoisting their wishable omens.

The rough of heaven clings to them
and cannot flee, eliding.

Finally,
she will make her way home, a sparrow

in a rookery, familiar—all this to wake her
from her light coma.

I would suggest the room with twin-light
faces—

where the wall jags, where the old wood
blessed be the world she knew

survives in nudges.

The Moonlight House

One thing I ask, one thing I seek,
To dwell in Yahweh's house.

Forget the witching mirror, the night's
bobeche, the constellation on the floor—

             the moon is rock,
with pocks and pockets of manmade boots;

the moon is earthen as David's mud:
slingshot and hope,

the placid flag, the unwhispered footprints.
From way below, a red fence

draws the bare vicinity into our eyes.
            Yet all I know are houses, here,

where every poem is house—the verbs
in rooms; the other words

in hampers, bins, or closets cueing.
I go through these, for one more treasure

between walls.
There—who recalls—at last, an altar and

an altar-bird, a workman, gold
and barefoot, disassembling tricky cages

one by one. His shoes are propped,
the heel-rise bent, the instep-flute electrified.

        I think him there—
call this a firmament or a tomb; the moon,

miraculous or amuck.
            Good God, where are you?

The knob again; a neighbor steals, insists:
between the kitchen and the windswept hall,

between the table where our hands culled
cumin, and night

unfilling through the passage-door.
           His knuckles bleed over the latch-

and-key, and moonlight binds them.

River Saint

We cannot ask
for resting place, or wish
for apse in church;
the martyr's eye, serene

as stone, forgot to claim
a grotto when we heaved and
hauled this Santo out of mud.
We went half-mad—

the sight of it;
    quick,
    Santo, Santo, pour
    your blessings on our banks.

We saw (how strange)
that the flood had missed
his crown, a smooth and
solid baldspot bound to rock.

We dipped our hands.
    With water we baptize.
But the saint, unblessed and
barren, fell from us, loosening

purple algae and cold rust,
his sacred mudskin petrified
as old Franciscan sack.
He tilted right, then farther,

farthest inland, ghost on grass;
who knows why saints and
mornings always rise, so
dangerously dry.

                      —*for Rowena S.*

Waters

Deep is calling to deep
by the roar of your cataracts,
all your waves and breakers
have rolled over me.

When it rains, we dream
of aging with one body, creatures
out of wondrous sac,

whirl of fists, flesh glowing,
gladdened in their pond.
We would pour intently edgeward,

all our marbled, eeling body
easing out entirely drenched.
There is, too, a dream of wrinkles

(those we call crowfeet, and fear)
crowding gently, flocked to flower
on our skin—

the result of so much water,
hours of dipping into grace, too long
for our good.

Perhaps we are not prepared
individually for this liquefied,
invasive light, meddling with a peel

too fine, stretched thin in our falling.
When we bathe and then forget,
slumberous in lukewarm basin

(wash, wash utterly all sin), the skin
puckers, crawls, crimps,
puddles awkwardly in every pore—

Has our dreaming come to this?
Do we shiver from too much life,
whine when water rises,

hold our breath afraid to drown,
dangle feet over the tepid tub,
drag the towel from the rack,

opting for its prickle?
      When it rains, the body asks
for lacum, lake, loch, lac, laguna...

babbling in one native tongue.
And it makes the bathers mad, slipping
over marble tiles, back to hazard

holiness—
      hallowed is our flood.

Saints in the Garden

I thought I'd break the secret to you now,
that in our yard a saint has set aside

his rucksack and a ruby glass of wine.
He's blonde, and at his side a hunchback leans,

kind smile and beard....
        They've come to honey up our walls,

our brickwork and our lamps,
and hang about as hummingbirds and plums.

          You don't believe me (in sanity,
who would) but there's a lily martyr

at the door, she might have been a Roman—
I don't know, except for all her tresses, the red

grapes: Agnes, perhaps; a lambkin's at her breast.
        Ah, humor me and trust—

although you say that visions are a trick
to stun the blow of dying,

the distress in our remaining bodies.
This nightly tease, you claim, exhausts the death-

wish of a lover at the soil, or of a mother tidying
a bib—so cold, so clinging.

            Does no one
ever show up at your gate—ghosts tucking used

aromas up their sleeves and sniffing out old
stories?   Seed-stone, rib-cradle, half-belief

in saints abiding, gleaming at the fence.
I'll say again: they peep in, push and wedge, widen

my glance—as masquerades, a feast; or thoughts,
a life. Or awe, that silver negative that yields

the changeless sky, the changing gist of trees.

A Way Through Words

No utterance at all, no speech;
not a sound to be heard—

Now and in the hour:
after this, a temporary silence—come, let the air fall gently

on our laps, as if a fleece uncurling, nothing
else, as if a lamb we choose out of a herd, the sacramental.

After our histories of speech—harangues in song and stammer
with notices alighting on the trees—lean back: umber and

ancient on the chair, our trembling carriage.
Of hopes, this is the most unbearable yet true, our hardest moment.

After the tidying up of prayers, *Heart*, at the first,
Amen against the last exhaling, we're asked to finger quietness,

to flick the sediments of sound away, as one would sweep
a desert. Ah, dry against dry, the dust lured into puffs, the mouth

of nature: strong is the tongue that tastes.
Now and in the hour—

    One murmur—
And we've left this temporary silence, voices racing to tell us

what things are like.   By rumoring, we raise the dead.
Blest be the word at stake, the universe of stars,

                articulate as childbirth.

Acknowledgments

My appreciation to the Virginia Commission for the Arts whose Poetry Fellowship Grant greatly facilitated the completion of this manuscript. Thanks are further owed to those publications where some of the poems, or variations of poems in this book, first appeared:

"Distances" in *American Literary Review*

"A Way Through Words" in *The Anglican Theological Review*

"The Dresser, on a Milky Morning" in *Bellevue Literary Review*

"Nightlife" in *Blackbird*

"The Moonlight House" in *Christianity and Literature*

"Lola's Window" in *A Commerce of Moments* (Pavement Saw Press)

"Intercession II" (as "Erato") in *Ginosko*

"Outlasting" in *Green Hills Literary Lantern*

"First House" and "Provinces" in *Hotel Amerika* ("Provinces" was First Prize winner at the 2004 Conference on Christianity and Literature Poetry Contest.)

"Migrations" in *The Madison Review*

"The Rood of Jesse", "Fiction", and "The House That Bled" in *The Marlboro Review* ("The House That Bled" won Editor's Prize in the 2002 Marlboro Prize in Poetry.)

"Adolescent", "The Armoire", "A Way With Words", and "The Scarf" in *Notre Dame Review*

"Leaving Pompeii" (as "Celebration") in *No Roses Review*

"All Souls Day" in *Pavement Saw Magazine*

"The Fret of Memory" in *Runes: A Review of Poetry*

"A Might-be Summer" and "La Flor de Tía Petíng" in *Potomac Review*

"The Monument Restorer" in *Southern Poetry Review*

"River Saint" in *Willow Review*

"Waters" (as "A Poem for Single Flesh. Part XIV") in *The 80ᵗʰ Anniversary Anthology of the Poetry Society of Virginia,* and in the chapbook, *Corpus Homini: A Poem for Single Flesh* (Wings Press)

"Marie's Heights" in *Roses So Red and Lilies So Fair,* Songs and Poems of Virginia, Created and Directed by Robert Arthur, Poetry Society of Virginia Annual Festival

---

Except where noted otherwise, the epigraphs that appear with the poems are derived from the Psalter.

About the Author

S **ofia M. Starnes** was born in Manila and educated in Madrid. She arrived in the United States in 1986 and became a U.S. citizen in 1989. Her publications include *The Soul's Landscape* (Aldrich, 2002), co-winner of the Aldrich Chapbook Poetry Award, judged by Billy Collins, and *A Commerce of Moments* (Pavement Saw Press, 2003), Editor's Choice in the Transcontinental Poetry Book Prize and a Poetry Honor Book in the Library of Virginia Literary Awards Competition. Her most recent collection, *Corpus Homini,* won the 2008 Wings Press Whitebird Chapbook Series competition. Her poems and essays have also appeared in numerous literary journals, including *Hayden's Ferry, Laurel Review, Notre Dame Review, Gulf Coast, Southern Poetry Review, Marlboro Review,* and *Pleiades.*

Starnes's poetry has been recognized in a variety of ways. She is the recipient of a poetry fellowship from the Virginia Commission for the Arts, the Rainer Maria Rilke Poetry Award, the Marlboro Poetry Award (Editor's Choice), the Christianity and Literature Poetry Prize, and a Pushcart Prize nomination, among other citations. She serves as poetry editor of *The Anglican Theological Review.* Sofia Starnes lives in Williamsburg, Virginia, with her husband Bill.